Felix Mendelssohn–Bartholdy
(1809–1847)

Songs without Words

Romances sans paroles

Lieder ohne Worte

III

for piano • pour piano • für Klavier

K 316

6 Lieder ohne Worte, Op. post. 85

1. Andante espressivo — 5
2. Allegro agitato — 8
3. Presto — 10
4. Andante sostenuto — 14
5. Allegretto — 18
6. Allegretto con moto, *sempre cantabile* — 20

Appendix 1

Lied ohne Worte, Op. 85, No. 1, Variant of C4 & C5
Andante — 23

Lied ohne Worte, Op. 85, No. 2, Variant of AU2
Allegro di molto — 26

Lied ohne Worte, Op. 85, No. 2, Variant of C4 & C5
Allegro agitato — 28

Lied ohne Worte, Op. 85, No. 3, Variant of AU3/II
Molto allegro — 30

Lied ohne Worte, Op. 85, No. 4, Variant of AU4/I
Andante — 34

Lied ohne Worte, Op. 85, No. 6, Variant of AU6/I
Andante quasi Allegretto, *assai leggiero* — 37

6 Lieder ohne Worte, Op. post. 102

1. Andante, un poco agitato — 42
2. Andante — 46

Kinderstück

3. Presto — 48

4. Andante un poco agitato — 51

Kinderstück

5. Allegro vivace — 54

6. Andante — 58

Appendix 2

Lied ohne Worte, Op. 102, No. 2, Version of AU2/I

Adagio — 60

11 Lieder ohne Worte

Lied ohne Worte in Es, LoO 1

1. Espressivo & Allegro — 62

[Lied ohne Worte] in A, LoO 2

2. Andante con moto — 64

[Lied ohne Worte] in A, LoO 3

3. Andante — 66

Lied ohne Worte in fis, LoO 4

4. Allegro molto — 67

[Lied ohne Worte] Album Blatt in e, LoO 5

5. Allegro — 72

[Lied ohne Worte] in A, LoO 6

6. — 80

Gondellied in A, LoO 7

7. Allegretto non troppo — 84

Ein Lied ohne Worte in F, LoO 8

8. — 86

[Lied ohne Worte] in a, LoO 9

9. Allegretto — 88

Reiter – Lied in d, LoO 10

10. Allegro vivace — 91

[Lied ohne Worte] in A, LoO 11
„Auf fröhliches Wiedersehen"

11. Allegro moderato — 94

6 Lieder ohne Worte
Heft VII, Op. post. 85
First publication: Bonn, 1851

Op. 85, No. 1
04. Apr. 1846

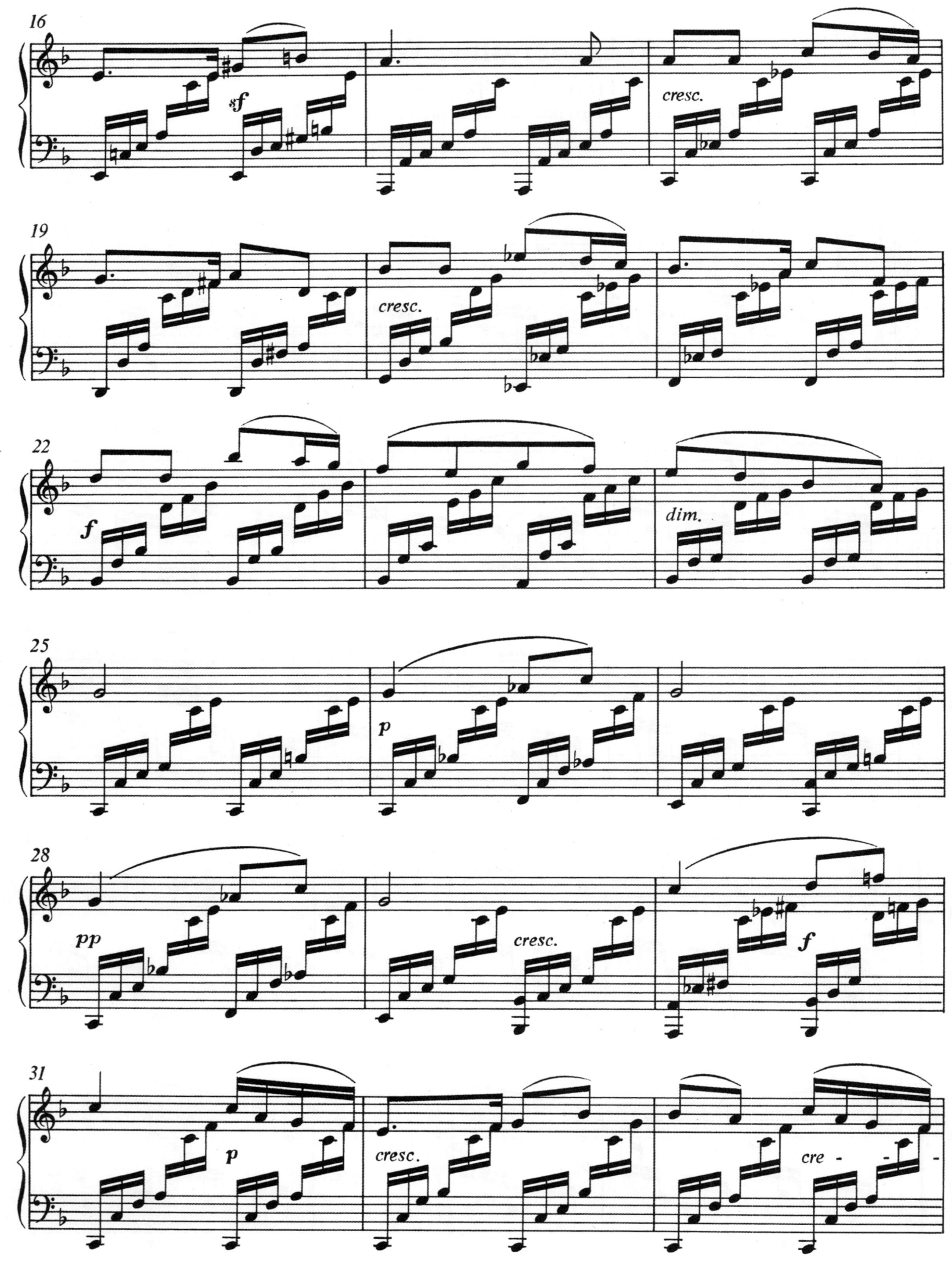

Op. 85, No. 3
04. Apr. 1846

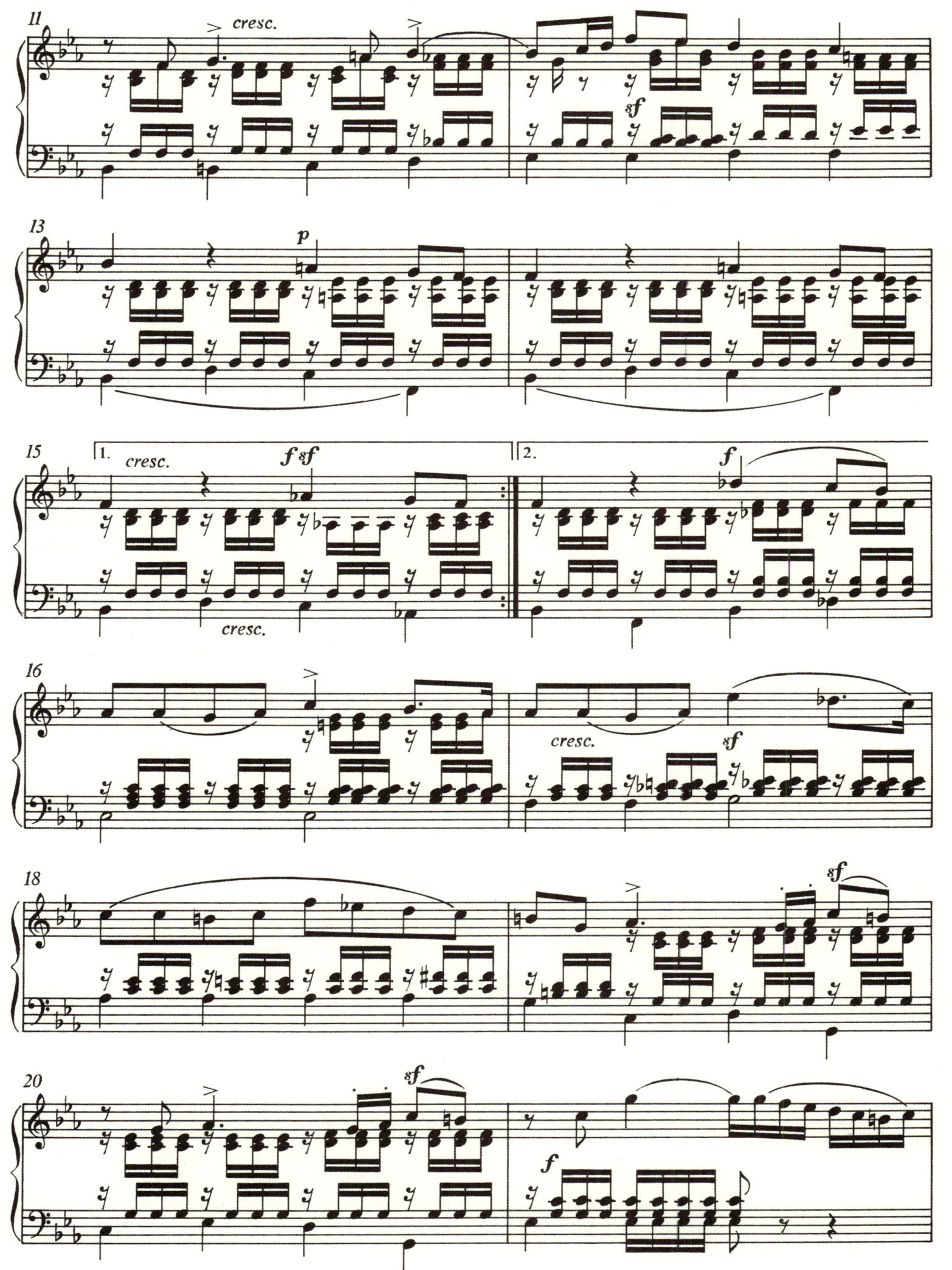

Lied ohne Worte, Op. 85, No. 5. Version of AU5.
KBJ, Mendelssohn Aut. 40, p. 54.

Op. 85, No. 5
04. Apr. 1846

Appendix 1

Lied ohne Worte

Op. 85, No. 1
Variant of C4 & C5
24. Dec. 1844 – 13. Jan. 1845

Lied ohne Worte

Op. 85, No. 2
Variant of AU2
09. June 1834

Lied ohne Worte

Op. 85, No. 2
Variant of C4&C5
24.Dec.1844–13.Jan.1845

An Henriette Grabau

Lied ohne Worte

Op. 85, No. 3
Variant of AU3/II
29. Mar. 1836

Lied ohne Worte

Op. 85, No. 4
Variant of AU4/I
03. May 1845, Frühfassung

[Lied ohne Worte]

Op. 85, No. 6
Variant of AU6/I
01. May 1841, Frühfassung

6 Lieder ohne Worte
Heft VIII, Op. post. 102
First publication: Bonn, 1868

Op. 102, No. 1
London, 01. June 1842

Lied ohne Worte, Op. 102, No. 2. Version of AU2/II.
KBJ, Mendelssohn Aut. 40, p. 56.

Op. 102, No. 2
Frankfurt, 11. May 1845

Kinderstück

Op. 102, No. 3
12. Dec. 1845

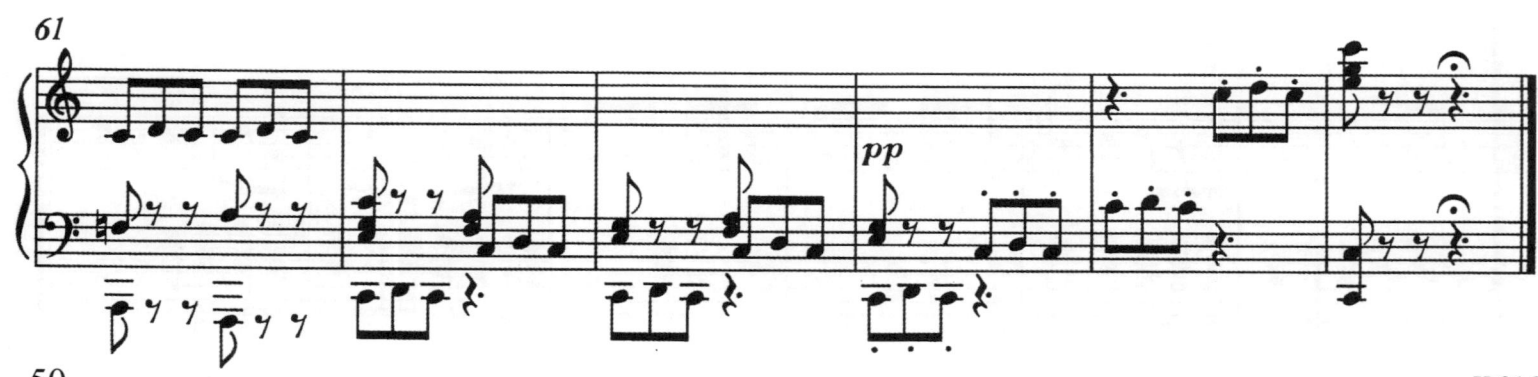

Op. 102, No. 4
04.Feb.1841

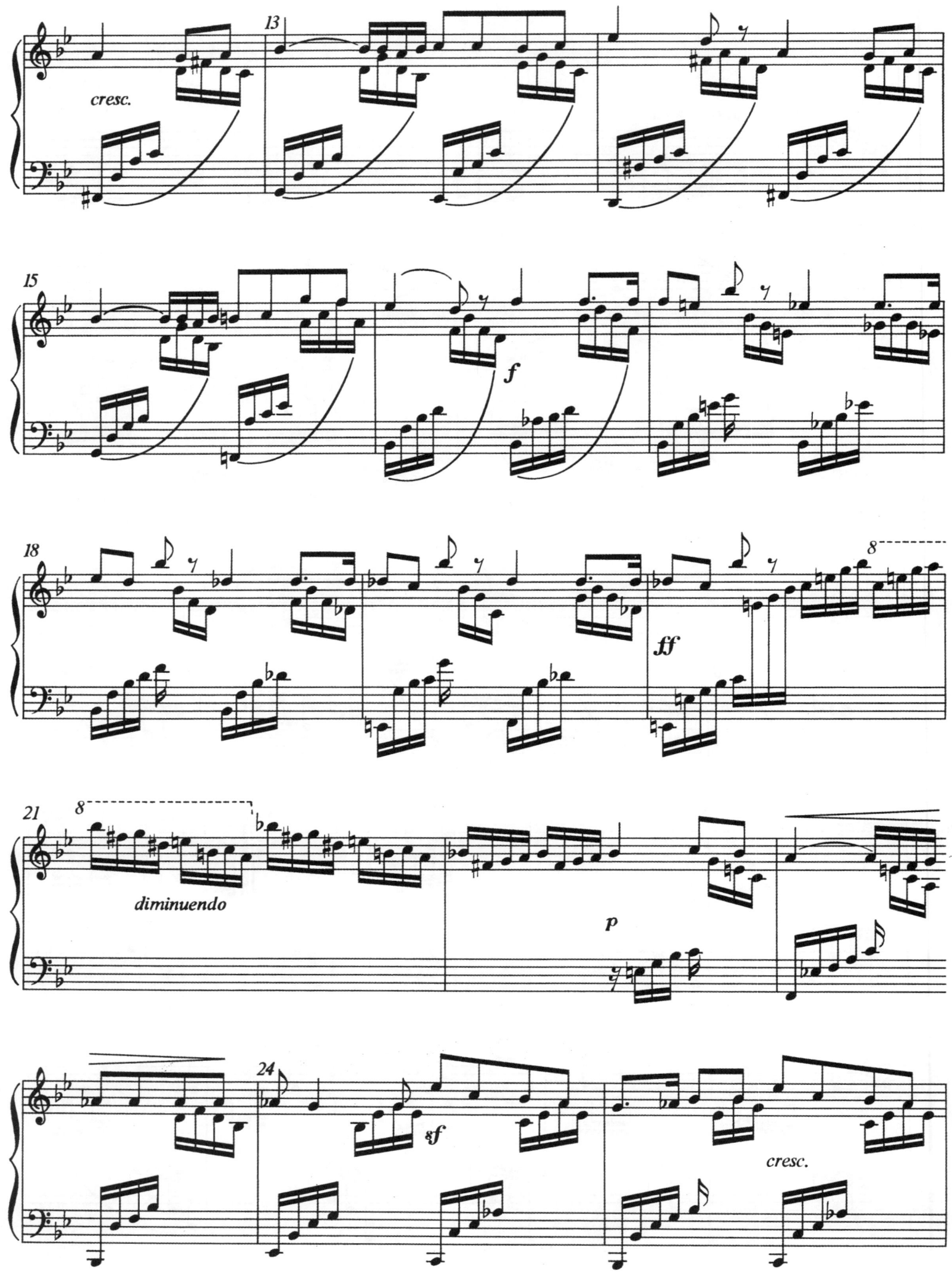

Kinderstück

Op. 102, No. 5
Leipzig, 12. Dec. 1845

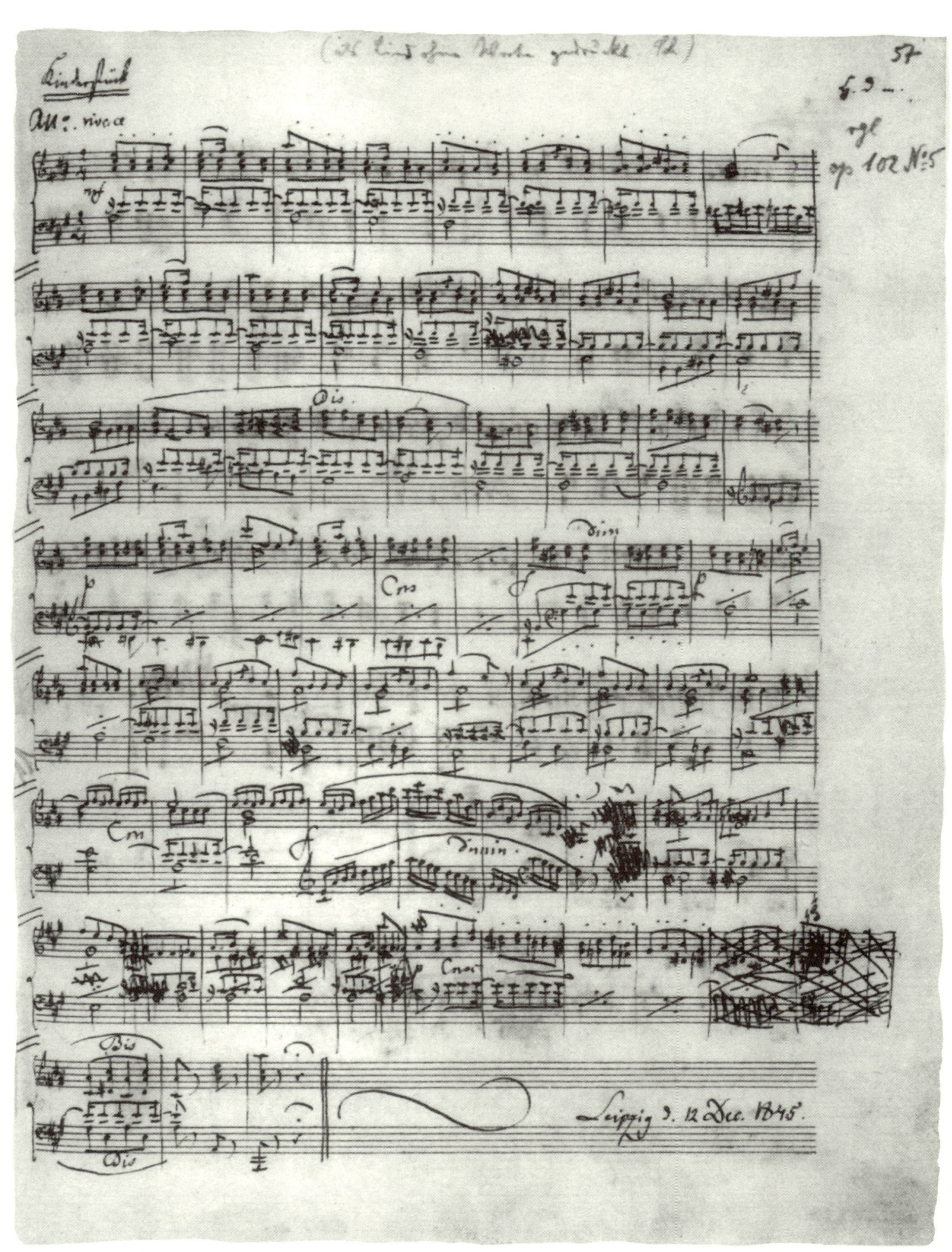

Lied ohne Worte, Op. 102, No. 5. Version of AU5.
KBJ, Mendelssohn Aut. 40, p. 57.

Op. 102, No. 6
05.Jul.1842

Appendix 2

Lied ohne Worte

Op. 102, No. 2
Version of AU2/I
25. May 1845

11 Lieder ohne Worte

Lied ohne Worte in Es

LoO 1
14. Nov. 1828

[Lied ohne Worte] in A

LoO 2
21.May–03.June 1830

[Lied ohne Worte] in A

LoO 3
13. June 1830

Lied ohne Worte in fis

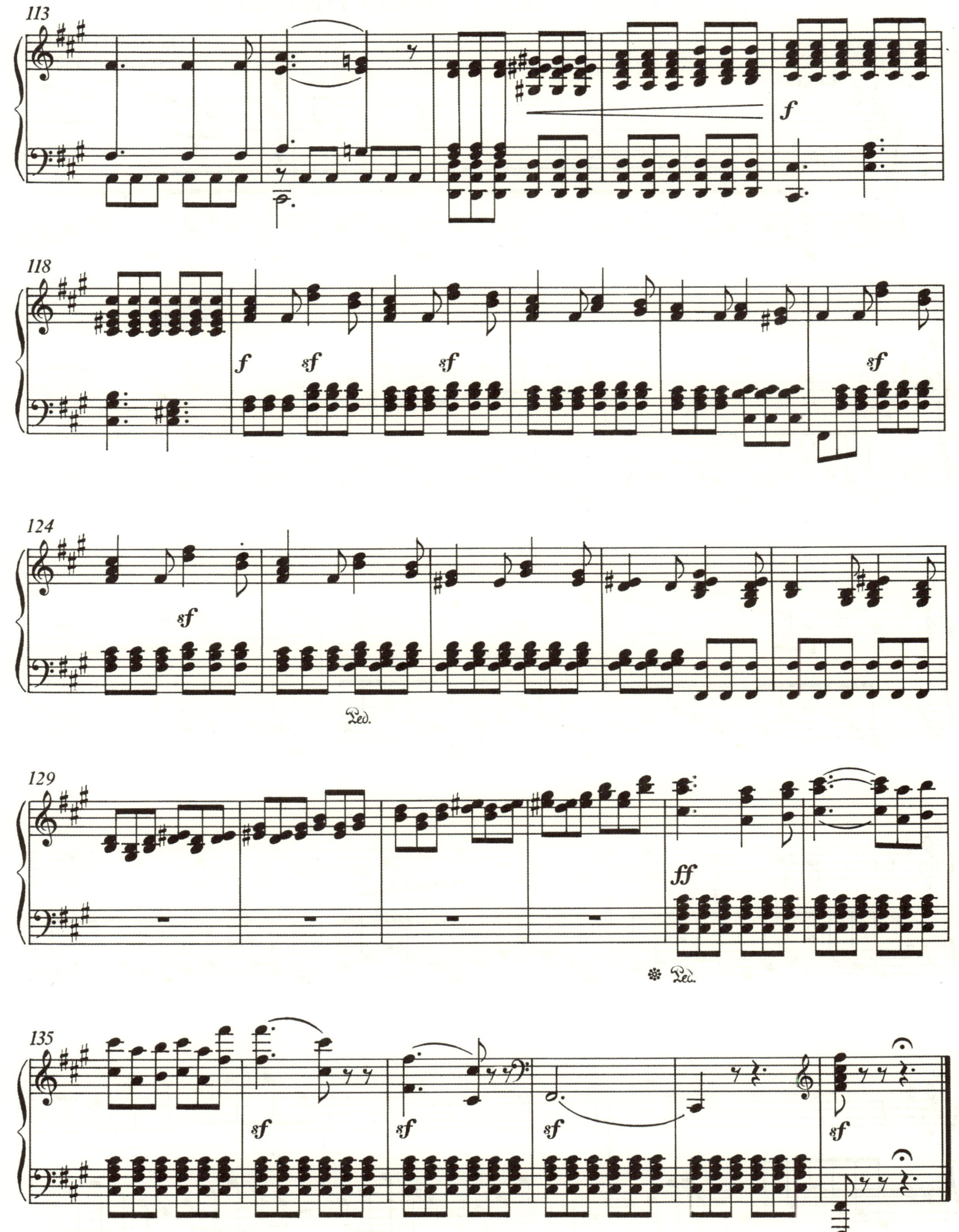

[Lied ohne Worte] Album Blatt in e

Op. post. 117, LoO 5
Frankfurt, 1836

[Lied ohne Worte] in A. LoO 6. Version of AU/I.
SBPK, Mus. ms. autogr. F. Mendelssohn Bartholdy 29, pp. 53–54.

[Lied ohne Worte] in A

LoO 6
22. Apr. 1837

Gondellied in A

LoO 7
03.Feb.1837

[Lied ohne Worte] in a

LoO 9
[ca. 1840–42]

[Lied ohne Worte] in a, LoO 9.
OBL, MS. M. Deneke Mendelssohn d. 60, No. 5, fol. 7ᵛ.

Reiter–Lied in d

LoO 10
12.Dec.1844–18.Dec.1846

OVER 25.000 PAGES OF PIANO MUSIC SHEETS ONLINE

Bach, Beethoven, Brahms, Chopin, Czerny, Debussy, Gershwin, Dvořák, Grieg, Haydn, Joplin, Lyadov, Mendelssohn-Bartholdy, Mozart, Mussorgsky, Purcell, Schubert, Schumann, Scriabin, Tchaikovsky and many more

KÖNEMANN

© 2018 koenemann.com GmbH
www.koenemann.com

Editor: István Máriássy
Responsible co-editor: Tamás Záskaliczky
Technical editor: Dezső Varga
Engraved by Kottamester Bt., Budapest

ISBN 978-3-7419-1484-3

Printed in China by Reliance Printing